T0198996

WHAT COLOR IS MY DAY?

MARCIA KASABACH

What Color is My Day ?

Hey, Hey, Hey !
What color is my day?

A simple change of color

Can brighten up my day.

I choose one for the mood I want

And chase out gloomy grey.

Blue is my color for today

Like a soothing summer breeze

Safe and calm and warm inside

I'm peaceful and at ease.

Maybe I'll choose Orange

Like flowers, bright and snappy.

It makes me smile and even laugh

I'm tickled and I'm happy.

Oh Purple! - I am Special
Like a Queen or like a King.
Strong and brave and confident
I can do anything!

There's vibrant, lively Red!

Like fire, excitement and heat

I want to skip and dance around

And feel the music's beat.

Or Pink - a quiet, dreamy mood

My imagination floating free

Like puffy clouds up in the sky

With wondrous shapes to see.

I choose my special color

Today it's just for me.

Did I forget a favorite one?

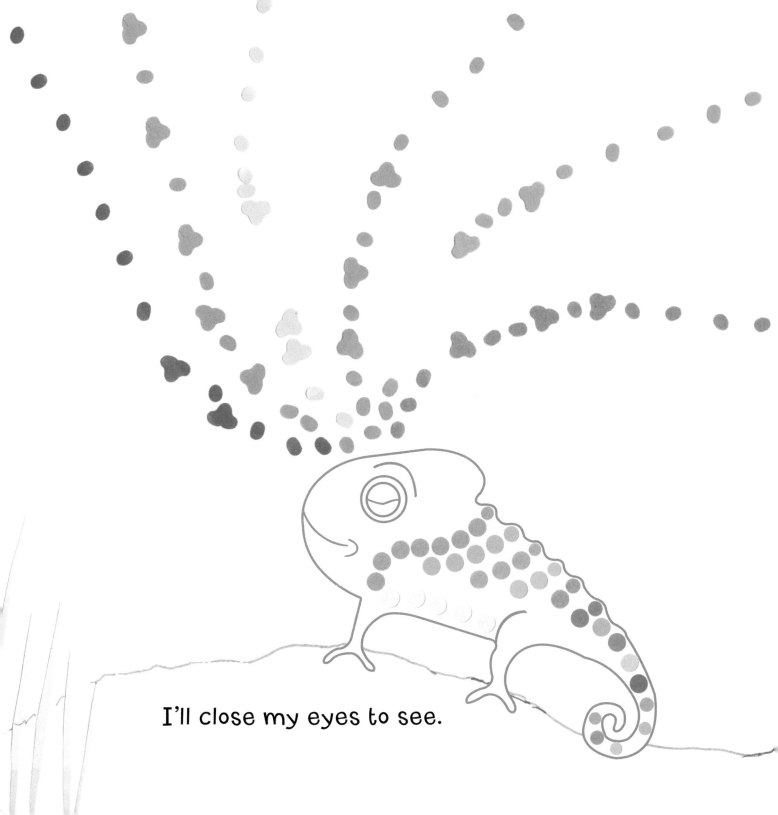

I'll close my eyes to see.

Oh yes, I see warm Yellow

Like sunshine, bold and bright

I want to play with friends today,

Sharing, laughing with delight.

I might want Green, fresh and new

Ready to explore and grow,

Unfolding like a baby leaf

So much I want to learn and know.

And even when I'm angry

Or grumpy, hurt or sad,

I imagine blue or yellow

To change and not feel bad.

It's easy to change colors.

I do it in a blink.

I sit real still and close my eyes.

It changes how I think.

I choose my color for today

It surrounds me like a bubble.

It comes with me wherever I go

To keep out any trouble.

Tomorrow might be different.

And yesterday is over.

Today is special, just for now.

Full of my favorite color.

Parent's Note - and for children of all ages.

Energy is real. It moves and changes.

Colors are one way to visualize, imagine and see energy.

A color can represent anything you want.

Try it.

What color is your day?

for Roan, Tessa, Alexa, Austin, Dela, Gabi & Nikki.

Thank You
Nikki & Dela Longfish for your invaluable
technical & professional assistance.
Lewis Bostwick for creating 'psychic kindergarten',
where I learned about energy - to see it and change it.

Balboa Press books may be ordered through booksellers or by contacting:

Balboa Press
A Division of Hay House
1663 Liberty Drive
Bloomington, IN 47403
www.balboapress.com
1 (877) 407-4847

The views expressed in this work are solely those of the author and do not necessarily reflect
the views of the publisher, and the publisher hereby disclaims any responsibility for them.

ISBN: 978-1-5043-9059-0 (sc)
ISBN: 978-1-5043-9060-6 (e)

Library of Congress Control Number: 2017916135

Print information available on the last page.

Balboa Press rev. date: 10/23/2017

BALBOA
PRESS
A DIVISION OF HAY HOUSE

Printed in the United States
By Bookmasters